Patterning Techniqu[es]

A pattern is a repetition of shapes and line[s]
depending on your preference and the spac[e you w]...
patterns start out very simple with either a line or a shape.

Repeating shapes (floating)

Shapes and lines are the basic building blocks of patterns. Here are some
example shapes that we can easily turn into patterns:

Before we turn these shapes into patterns, let's spruce them up a bit by outlining,
double-stroking (going over a line more than once to make it thicker), and
adding shapes to the inside and outside.

To create a pattern from these embellished shapes, all you have to do is repeat
them, as shown below. You can also add small shapes in between the embellished
shapes, as shown.

These are called "floating"
patterns because they are not
attached to a line. These floating
patterns can be used to fill space
anywhere and can be made big
or small, short or long, to suit
your needs.

Tip

If you add shapes and patterns to
these coloring pages using pens
or markers, make sure the ink is
completely dry before you color
on top of them; otherwise, the ink
may smear.

Coloring Techniques & Media

My favorite way to color is to combine a variety of media so I can benefit from the best that each has to offer. When experimenting with new combinations of media, I strongly recommend testing first by layering the colors and media on scrap paper to find out what works and what doesn't. It's a good idea to do all your testing in a sketchbook and label the colors/brands you used for future reference.

Markers & colored pencils

Smooth out areas colored with marker by going over them with colored pencils. Start by coloring lightly, and then apply more pressure if needed.

marker   +   colored pencil   =   smoother result

Test your colors on scrap paper first to make sure they match. You don't have to match the colors if you don't want to, though. See the cool effects you can achieve by layering a different color on top of the marker below.

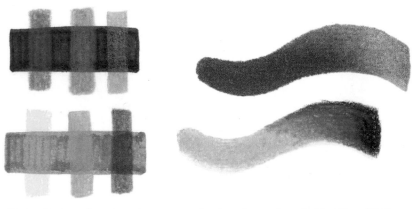

Markers (horizontal) overlapped with colored pencils (vertical).

Purple marker overlapped with white and light blue colored pencils. Yellow marker overlapped with orange and red colored pencils.

Markers & gel pens

Markers and gel pens go hand in hand, because markers can fill large spaces quickly, while gel pens have fine points for adding fun details. White gel pens are especially fun for drawing over dark colors, while glittery gel pens are great for adding sparkly accents.

Color Theory

Check out this nifty color wheel. Each color is labeled with a P (primary), S (secondary), or T (tertiary). The **primary colors** are red, yellow, and blue. They are "primary" because they can't be created by mixing other colors. Mixing primary colors creates the **secondary colors** orange, green, and purple (violet). Mixing a primary and a secondary color creates the **tertiary colors** yellow-orange, yellow-green, blue-green, blue-purple, red-purple, and red-orange.

Working toward the center of the six large petals, you'll see three rows of lighter colors, called tints. A **tint** is a color plus white. Moving in from the tints, you'll see three rows of darker colors, called shades. A **shade** is a color plus black.

The colors on the top half of the color wheel are considered **warm** colors (red, yellow, orange), and the colors on the bottom half are called **cool** (green, blue, purple).

Colors opposite one another on the color wheel are called **complementary**, and colors that are next to each other are called **analogous**.

Look at the examples and note how each color combo affects the overall appearance and "feel" of the butterfly on the next page. For more inspiration, check out the colored examples on the following pages. Refer to the swatches at the bottom of the page to see the colors selected for each piece.

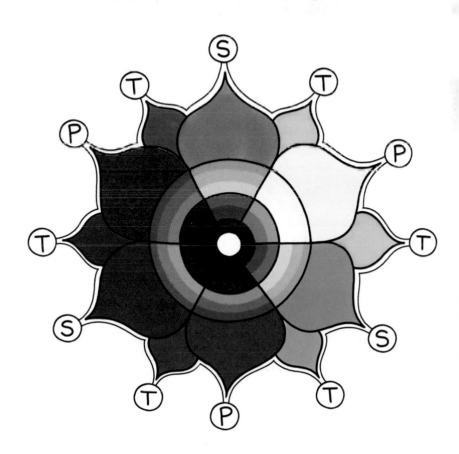

Warm colors

Cool colors

Warm colors with cool accents

Cool colors with warm accents

Tints and shades of red

Tints and shades of blue

Analogous colors

Complementary colors

© Thaneeya McArdle • www.thaneeya.com

Color by Ranae Davidson.

Color by Catherine Ryan.

Color by Kati Erney.

Color by Cindy Fahs.

Never worry about the size of your Christmas tree. In the eyes of children, they are all 30 feet tall.

—Larry Wilde

_____
_____
_____
_____
_____
_____
_____
_____
_____
_____
_____

© Thaneeya McArdle • www.thaneeya.com

When it seems that we have lost our way
We find ourselves again on Christmas Day.

—Believe

First we'll make snow angels for two hours, then we'll go ice skating, then we'll eat a whole roll of Tollhouse cookie dough as fast as we can, and then we'll snuggle.

—Elf

_____

_____

_____

_____

_____

_____

_____

_____

_____

_____

Frosty the snowman
Was a jolly happy soul
With a corncob pipe and a button nose
And two eyes made out of coal

—*Frosty the Snowman*

_____
_____
_____
_____
_____
_____
_____
_____
_____
_____
_____

Christmas time is here
Happiness and cheer
Fun for all that children call
Their favorite time of the year

—Christmas Time Is Here

_____

_____

_____

_____

_____

_____

_____

_____

_____

_____

It is Christmas in the heart that puts
Christmas in the air.

—W. T. Ellis

_____

_____

_____

_____

_____

_____

_____

_____

_____

© Thaneeya McArdle • www.thaneeya.com

There is nothing in the world so irresistibly contagious as laughter and good humor.

—Charles Dickens, *A Christmas Carol*

Seeing isn't believing. Believing is seeing.

—*The Santa Clause*

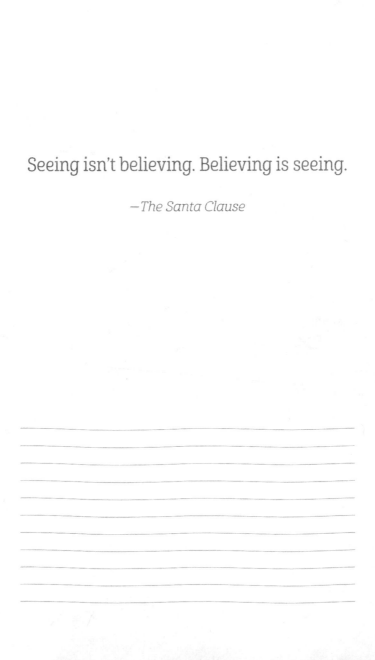

© Thaneeya McArdle • www.thaneeya.com

Christmas waves a magic wand over
this world, and behold, everything is softer
and more beautiful.

—Norman Vincent Peale

© Thaneeya McArdle • www.thaneeya.com

A balanced diet is a
Christmas cookie in each hand.

—Unknown

———————————————————————
———————————————————————
———————————————————————
———————————————————————
———————————————————————
———————————————————————
———————————————————————
———————————————————————
———————————————————————
———————————————————————

There's a certain magic that comes with the very first snow...For when the first snow is also a Christmas snow, well, something wonderful is bound to happen.

—*Frosty the Snowman*

_____
_____
_____
_____
_____
_____
_____
_____
_____
_____

Rocking around the Christmas tree
Let the Christmas spirit ring
Later we'll have some pumpkin pie
and we'll do some caroling

—Rockin' Around the Christmas Tree

I'll be home for Christmas
You can count on me
Please have snow and mistletoe
And presents under the tree

—I'll Be Home for Christmas

Every time a bell rings, an angel gets his wings.

—*It's a Wonderful Life*

I never thought it was such a bad little tree. It's not bad at all, really. Maybe it just needs a little love.

—*A Charlie Brown Christmas*

I will honor Christmas in my heart, and try to keep it all the year.

—Charles Dickens, *A Christmas Carol*

_____

_____

_____

_____

_____

_____

_____

_____

_____

_____

_____

Oh the weather outside is frightful,
But the fire is so delightful,
And since we've no place to go,
Let It Snow! Let It Snow! Let It Snow!

—Let It Snow

© Thaneeya McArdle • www.thaneeya.com

Gifts of time and love are surely the basic
ingredients of a truly merry Christmas.

—Peg Bracken

_____

_____

_____

_____

_____

_____

_____

_____

_____

Some people are worth melting for.

—Olaf, *Frozen*

© Thaneeya McArdle • www.thaneeya.com

If there is love in your heart and your mind
You will feel like Christmas all the time

—Where Are You Christmas?

Oh, Christmas isn't just a day, It's a frame of mind.

—*Miracle on 34th Street*

The snow is falling,
The city is white,
Your eyes are shining,
like diamonds tonight.

—98 Degrees, *This Gift*

_____

_____

_____

_____

_____

_____

_____

_____

_____

_____

_____

© Thaneeya McArdle • www.thaneeya.com

Jolly old Saint Nicholas, Lean your ear this way;
Don't you tell a single soul, what I'm going to say,
Christmas Eve is coming soon; Now, you dear old man,
Whisper what you'll bring to me; Tell me if you can.

—Jolly Old Saint Nicholas

_____

_____

_____

_____

_____

_____

_____

_____

_____

_____

Sleigh bells ring, are you listening?
In the lane, snow is glistening
A beautiful sight,
We're happy tonight,
Walking in a winter wonderland.

—Winter Wonderland

_____

_____

_____

_____

_____

_____

_____

_____

_____

All I want for Christmas is my two front teeth,
My two front teeth, See my two front teeth!
Gee, if I could only have my two front teeth,
Then I could wish you, "Merry Christmas."

—Donald Yetter Gardner,
All I Want For Christmas Is My Two Front Teeth

_____

_____

_____

_____

_____

_____

_____

_____

_____

I want a hippopotamus for Christmas
Only a hippopotamus will do
No crocodiles, no rhinoceros
I only likes hippopotamuses
And hippopotamuses like me, too

—I Want a Hippopotamus for Christmas

A toy is never truly happy
until it is loved by a child.

—Rudolf the Red-Nosed Reindeer

© Thaneeya McArdle • www.thaneeya.com

—Don't get your tinsel in a tangle!

—Unknown